the guide to owning a
Mouse

Sue Fox

T.F.H. Publications, Inc.
One TFH Plaza
Third and Union Avenues
Neptune City, NJ 07753

This book has been published with the intent to provide accurate and authoritative information in regard to the subject matter within. While every precaution has been taken in preparation of this book, the publisher and author assume no responsibility for errors or omissions. Neither is any liability assumed for damages resulting from the use of the information herein.

ISBN 0-7938-2155-X

www.tfh.com

Contents

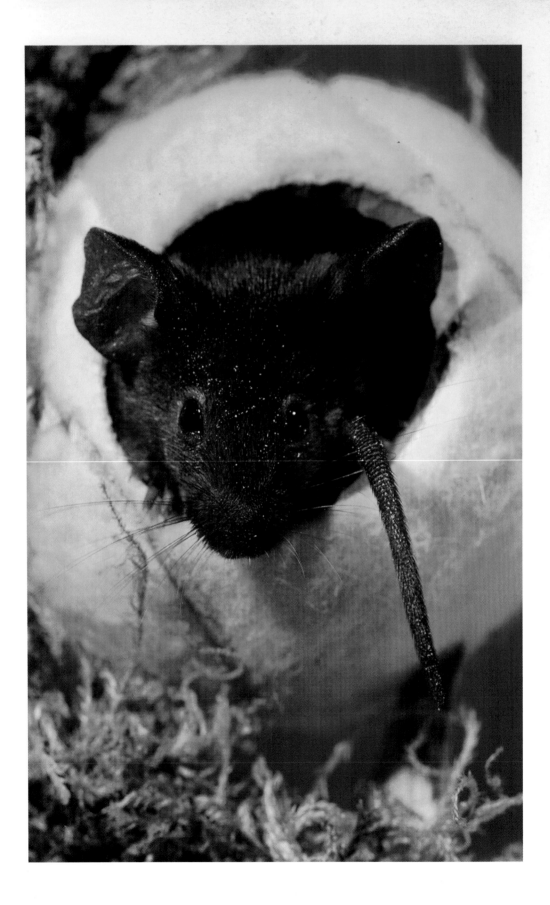

Introduction

MICE AS PETS

Mice can be delightful little pets. The species kept as a pet, the house mouse (*Mus musculus*), has a long history of association with people. Initially, mice were viewed as pests, because of the damage they inflicted on stored food and grain. However, people have a soft spot for mice, which are often seen as endearing, shy, and timid creatures, while their cousin the rat is usually thought of as sneaky and vicious.

People domesticated mice more than a hundred years ago, and because they have been bred in cap-

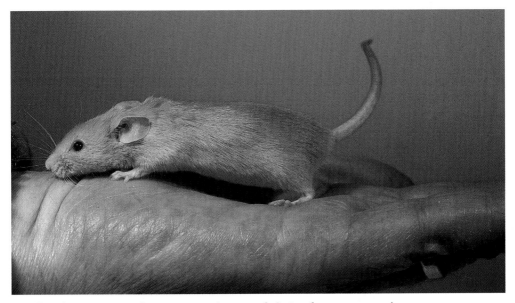

Small and easy to care for, mice are the pet of choice for many people.

Mice are inexpensive to purchase. Your local pet dealer can assist you when it comes to making a decision as to what type of mouse is best for you.

tivity for thousands of generations, domesticated mice are docile and easy to handle. Not counting their tail, mice measure fewer than four inches in length. Their small size appeals to adults and children who are captivated by the mouse's cute looks. Mice are inexpensive, undemanding, and easy to care for. Mice can be kept in their cage full-time as long as they are provided a spacious, entertaining (toy-filled) cage in which to play. They can be as relaxing to watch as an aquarium of tropical fish. Mice can even remain unattended in their cage over the weekend as long as they are given extra food and water.

Mice can be friendly and can learn that seeing their owner means food and playtime. Some tame mice will even come to their cage door to greet their owner. However, mice are not cuddly pets. They do not mind being petted, but they prefer to crawl around and investigate their surroundings rather than being cuddled for long periods of time. Pet mice typically bite only when they are afraid or threatened, but they are not aggressive animals. Gentle, regular handling will make your pet docile and reduce the likelihood of him ever biting you.

A pet mouse is very clean and performs an elaborate grooming ritual several times a day. The mouse first licks his front feet, then, using both front feet, he washes his face and behind his ears. Using his hind foot, the mouse delicately cleans the inside of his ears and then nibbles clean his

This female violet Dutch mouse will delight any owner with her mischievous behavior.

toes. The mouse continues washing the fur all over his body and then licks his hind toes after scratching with them. You will also see your pet mouse nibble clean his long tail. Mice are very fastidious, and many will even set up a separate toilet area in their cage.

LIFESPAN

Mice live between one-and-a-half years to three years of age. A short lifespan can be sad for pet owners who become attached to their mice. However, one advantage of the short life span is that mice do not live so long that children become uninterested in their pets. Longer-lived pets, such as rabbits, can be neglected by children or their adult owners once the novelty of owning the pet has worn off. Before you bring home a mouse, be sure that you are willing to commit to caring for your new pet for the rest of his lifetime.

SENSES AND SKILLS

Mice have some acute senses that help them to survive, but eyesight is not one of them. Mice have poor vision. They can detect little or no color so they see in various shades of gray. Bright light can damage a mouse's eyes. As you might guess, the eyes of albino mice are more sensitive to light than their dark-eyed counterparts. Mice naturally avoid bright lights because they are noctur-

nal, which means they are active at night.

Mice have an acute sense of hearing. They can communicate and hear sounds in the ultrasonic range, which people cannot hear. For the first two weeks of their life, baby mice communicate with their parents using ultrasonic sounds. Mice make ultrasonic calls when mating and fighting, as well as high-pitched squeaking sounds that people can hear.

A keen sense of smell helps mice locate food and detect pheromones used in social interactions. Pheromones are chemicals secreted from the body that facilitate communication and influence behavior between members of the same species. An example of this is territorial urine-marking. Male mice, in particular, mark their territory with urine and droppings, so that other male mice, especially younger males, will avoid the marked area. Mice also communicate with other mice through body language. For example, a mouse that wants to be groomed will crouch in front of another mouse, while a mouse that is challenging another mouse will assume a threatening stance.

A mouse's tail is covered with overlapping scales and fine fur. The mouse's tail helps him balance when he runs, sits on his haunches, and climbs. The scales can ruffle backward and give the mouse a good grip. A

There are many different color varieties of mice available in the hobby.

mouse can partially wrap his tail around an object to help him climb, but he cannot hang from his tail. A healthy young mouse usually carries his tail in the air to help his balance, but an old or sick mouse might drag his tail.

Mice use their whiskers to help them navigate. The whiskers that are found near the eyes, lips, and cheeks greatly aid a mouse as he wanders. When a mouse is scampering about, the whiskers on his cheeks perceive the horizontal and ground surfaces, while the ones above his eyes detect overhead surfaces.

Mice do not have sweat glands, nor can they pant like a dog to cool themselves off, so they are susceptible to overheating. However, both their tail and ears help them regulate their body temperature. When a mouse is cold, the blood vessels in his tail and ears constrict, which helps the mouse conserve heat. Cold mice also huddle and sleep together to conserve heat. When a mouse is hot, the vessels radiate heat to help the mouse cool off. By sprawling out away from each other when they are hot, the mice cool off even further.

TEETH

A mouse has two pairs of chisel-like incisors in the front of its mouth. These teeth never stop growing. The incisor teeth enable a mouse to carry nuts and other food items and to easily open hard seeds and nuts. A mouse's teeth are constantly worn down when he gnaws and chews on hard substances. If you look at a mouse's front teeth, you will notice that the lower incisors are up to three times longer than the upper incisors. Mice also have powerful jaw muscles and teeth. They can easily gnaw through the hard outer shell of a nut. The space between the incisors and the rear molars is called the diastema. When a mouse eats, his cheeks block this space to prevent any sharp food from being swallowed.

MICE AND CHILDREN

Owning a pet is one of the pleasures of childhood, however, parents cannot expect a young child to be solely responsible for a pet. To a varying extent, a parent must participate in the care of a child's pet. Such assistance might be driving to the pet store to buy fresh food, or reminders to feed the pet and clean the cage. Because young children cannot be expected to care for their pet without some supervision, it helps if a parent is enthusiastic about the pet. Unsupportive parents can make it more difficult for children to care for their pets. Simply by showing an interest in the animal, parents can encourage their child to care for the pet.

Children like to play with their pets. If a small pet struggles while being held, some children tend to squeeze harder instead of relaxing their grip. Sometimes this rough handling can frighten a mouse and cause him to bite. A parent can help reduce the risk of a bite by showing children how to properly hold the mouse and instructing them on what to do should their pet begin to wiggle. For example, a parent can teach the child to return the mouse to his cage if he no longer wants to be held. A parent might need to help take the mouse out of his cage for the child to visit with, or teach the child to open the cage and let the mouse come to him rather than pulling the mouse out of his home. Very young children always need to be supervised when they are playing with mouse or any other small pet.

Mice make fun and interesting pets for people of all ages. They are affectionate and show their attachment to their owners in their own unique ways.

Selecting a Mouse

BUYING A HEALTHY MOUSE

The premises of the pet store or breeder from where you buy your mice should be clean. While some smell is normal, if the odor in the store or the mice's cage is excessively pungent, buy your mice somewhere else. Check to be sure that the

When selecting a mouse as a pet, you should examine a few different mice. A healthy mouse is active and curious.

mice have enough food and clean water. An empty food dish or a dirty water bottle is a sign of poor care, and mice housed in these conditions are less likely to be healthy.

A healthy mouse should have dense, shiny fur. The coat should be smooth and sleek with no bald areas or flaky skin. The mouse's eyes should be clear and bright. Your choice should look solid and a little plump. A healthy mouse should not have an easily detected protruding backbone. Do not choose a mouse that is listless, sneezes, has runny eyes or a runny nose, a rough or thin coat, lumps, or scabs. Dirty, matted fur near a mouse's tail could be a sign of diarrhea.

Choose your mouse from a clean, uncrowded cage. Mice that come from a dirty, crowded environment are less likely to be healthy. No matter how much you might like a particular mouse or want to buy a pet mouse that day; do not buy a mouse if any of the mice in a cage exhibit symptoms of ill health. Although the mouse you want might appear healthy, he has been exposed to sick mice and is likely to become ill at a later time, often triggered by the stress of going to a new home. The staff at the pet store should be able to answer any questions you have about mice and their care.

A healthy mouse is active and curious. He should not limp or move awkwardly. A good choice is a mouse that is inquisitive and investigates your hand when you place it in the cage. A mouse that sniffs your hand and runs away, but returns to further investigate you, will also make a good pet. Do not choose a mouse that runs and hides, struggles frantically, or is aggressive and tries to bite.

Pick a young mouse, since it will be easier to tame and will most likely live longer than an older mouse. Mice are weaned from their mother at about three to four weeks of age, but they should not be moved into a new home until they are at least five weeks of age. The best time to buy your mice is when they are between five to eight weeks old and about two to three inches in body length.

Avoid buying recently weaned babies because they are easily stressed and more susceptible to illness. Some pet stores will know the age of the mice you are considering buying. If they do not, use other criteria to determine the mouse's age. A mouse that is too young will have a head that looks too large for his body, his fur might not be smooth and glossy, and he will often move by playful hops rather than walking.

FEEDER MICE VERSUS PET MICE

Mice can be bought at pet stores or from hobbyists who breed fancy varieties, often for mice shows. Most pet stores carry mice, and many mice are

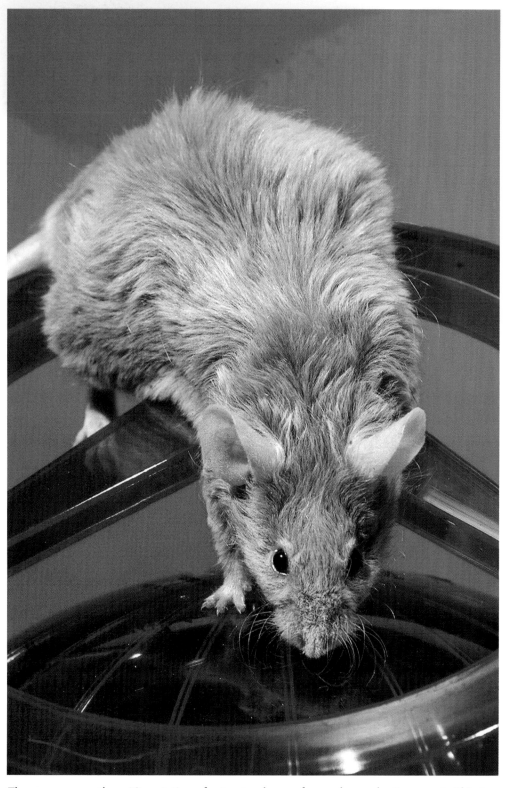

There are more than 40 varieties of mice to choose from when selecting a pet. This is a dove rex mouse.

sold as "feeders" for pet snakes and lizards. The best pet stores will house their feeder mice in separate cages from their pet mice. You do not want a feeder mouse as a pet. Feeder mice are bred in large numbers and are often less healthy and typically less friendly than mice bred specifically for pets. Because feeder mice are food for reptiles, the breeders who produce feeder mice do not need to be concerned with the mice's temperament.

Pet stores usually keep their feeder mice in large numbers in a single cage because individual mice are continually being sold from the cage. Feeder mice are often all one color, such as albino or agouti. Mice bred and sold as pets are usually colorful and should not be kept in large numbers in a single cage.

SHOWING MICE

Although you might find it surprising, mice are exhibited in shows just like dogs, cats, and horses. The mice are judged by experts who determine how closely the mice conform to the ideal standard for shape, appearance, color, or markings. (The many varieties of fancy mice are discussed in the following section.) Of most importance to potential pet-mice owners, the show mouse must be docile and easy to handle. Mice that are nervous, timid, or try to bite are penalized and are less likely to win awards. Hobbyists who show their mice preferentially breed mice that have won awards, thus mice with undesirable temperaments are less likely to be bred. Because temperament has a hereditary component, show mice bred by hobbyists tend to have better pet qualities (for example, they are confident, not nervous) than randomly obtained mice whose heredity is unknown. You can find hobbyists who breed fancy varieties of mice in the advertisement section of pet magazines and Internet sites devoted to pet fancy mice.

VARIETIES

Fancy mice come in more than 40 varieties. Similar to breeds of cat, the different varieties of mice differ from each other in color, markings, coat textures, and sometimes temperament. Besides the standard wild agouti color, mice are available in dozens of attractive colors, including black, gold, orange, red, cream, fawn, silver, blue, and chocolate. Mice come in solid colors (referred to by fanciers as "selfs"), a solid color with a tan or white belly (referred to as tan or fox), and marked, which includes mice with patches of color in various configurations such as Dutch, Himalayan (similar in looks to the Himalayan cat), banded, and variegated. Fancy mice can be found with the typical short sleek coat, or they can have long hair, satin hair (very attractive as the fur has a high glossy sheen), frizzy hair (wavy hair with curly whiskers), or they can be hairless. Their eyes are either pink or black.

All small animals kept in captivity eventually develop mutations from their standard color. In the wild, animals that are unusual in color are more noticeable to predators and often do not live long enough to reproduce. Hence, unusual colors are not typically found in wild populations. However, compared to their wild counterparts, house mice can come in unusual colors. White-colored mice were first recorded in historical Chinese and Roman documents more than a thousand years ago. Since then, hobbyists have increased the prevalence of color mutations by selectively breeding mice with desirable colors. As early as the 1700s, people in Japan were already breeding different colored varieties of mice. A British trader brought some of these varieties to Europe in the mid-19th century. Breeders in Europe formed clubs that helped to increase the popularity of fancy mice, especially in Great Britain.

By learning about genetics and carefully keeping track of the results of certain pairings, breeders are able to develop new mutations in color, coat length, and texture. Breeders attempt to "fix" the desirable trait by line breeding (for example, breeding a father with a daughter or a brother to sister). Due to inbreeding, line

Many pet stores do not stock a large variety of fancy mice. If you are looking for a particular variety, ask if it can be ordered or contact a breeder.

breeding can sometimes cause problems such as a shorter life span, greater susceptibility to health problems, or a more aggressive temperament with other mice. Should you ever choose to show mice, you eventually would want to learn more about the inheritance of color and coat types.

Pet stores usually do not stock a wide variety of fancy mice. If you have your heart set on a particular variety of mouse that proves hard to find, check whether a pet store can special order the mouse for you from their suppliers, or contact a breeder in your local area.

MORE THAN ONE?

A mouse can be kept by itself. However, mice are social animals. In the wild, they tend to live in extended family groups. A single mouse will be happier and more playful if he has a friend. Part of the fun in keeping pet mice is watching them wrestle and play as they take turns chasing each other around their cage. Two mice will also groom each other, especially in hard-to-reach places such as the neck and back, and curl up to sleep together. A mouse kept alone tends to be less active, sleeps more, and therefore, is less happy and less interesting. If, for some reason, you are set on getting only one mouse, plan on spending time playing with your pet several times a day.

Buy two young mice at the same time so they can grow up together. Two female mice get along best. Male mice will fight as they get older and often must be kept alone. However, some pet owners successfully keep male mice together when the mice are purchased as young littermate brothers. They must be provided with a large cage (at least two feet in length) that contains two separate nest boxes. If you choose a male and a female, they will produce babies every 20 to 36 days. Neutering the male mouse, which must be performed by a qualified veterinarian, will prevent the male from impregnating the female.

Mice are very social animals. Consider buying two mice so that they can keep each other company. They'll also keep you entertained as they play together.

Adult mice (about 12 weeks old) are territorial and will fight if an unfamiliar mouse is placed into their home. If one member of a pair dies, you can try to introduce another mouse. An adult mouse will more readily accept a younger mouse, but it might also attack the newcomer.

FEMALE OR MALE?

Female mice are called does, and male mice are called bucks. Male mice are larger than females and have a stronger "mousy" odor. Because males are smellier, many pet owners prefer female mice. Neutering will reduce the strong odor associated with male mice. This can be a relatively expensive option compared to the initial purchase price of the mouse, but it is money well spent if the only other option is finding a new home for a beloved pet due to a family member's complaints of smell.

Male mice also can be differentiated from females by the distance between their anus and their genital papilla, which is much greater in males than in females. An adult male's scrotum will also create a bulge near the base of his tail, though this is less easily detected in younger mice. The female has two rows of five nipples, but these can be difficult to see. You can more readily determine a mouse's gender by comparing it to the other mice in the cage. Ask a pet-store employee to help you determine the gender of your pets before you buy them.

Be aware that a female mouse might be pregnant if she was not separated soon enough from the males. Female mice can first breed at six weeks of age and male mice can begin breeding between six to eight weeks of age. After a gestation period of 19 to 21 days, the female mouse can give birth to between 4 to 12 babies. Baby mice are born pink and hairless, with their eyes closed, and they cannot be weaned from their mother until they are at least three weeks old. Because of the possibility of a female being pregnant, try to buy your mice from a pet store where the females are kept separate from the males.

If you decide to keep a male and female mouse together, you can expect your pets to have babies for the duration of the female's reproductive life, which is about one and a half years. While this can be fun and interesting, do consider whether you are able to find new homes for all the babies your pets will be making. Pet stores might be interested in buying some of them, but they might not always need mice when you are trying to find new homes for your weaned mice. If you are going to breed mice, consider choosing mice with the less common colors, as pet stores are often more interested in such varieties.

Some mice are better than others as house pets. Check with your pet dealer to make the best selection for an active mouse, rather than one that is shy around people.

BRINGING HOME YOUR NEW MOUSE

Ask the pet-store employee to place a small handful of shavings from the mice's original cage into the container you are using to take your mice home. Place the old shavings into your pets' new home. The smell of their original home can help your mice settle more comfortably into their new environment.

Before you buy your mice you should purchase their cage and supplies and have everything ready prior to bringing home your new pets. If your new pets' home is not yet set up for their occupancy, have someone else watch them while you arrange their new quarters. Mice can quickly chew out of the cardboard box pro-

vided by most pet stores for the trip home. Potential escapes are not a concern if you bring your mice home in a small, plastic animal carrier. Be sure to provide a dark, enclosed hide box for your mice within their carrying cage. Mice that have no place to hide will feel exposed and stressed and can take longer to settle into their new home.

When you first bring your mice home, they might be frightened and hide in their nest box. Some mice are more confident and will readily investigate their new home. Either way, let your new pets settle down and get used to their new home before you begin playing with them. Use this time to think of names for your new pets. Your mice will learn to associate their names with feeding and play time, and this will help you tame them. Some mice appear immediately comfortable in their new surroundings and will respond to your friendly attempts by crawling on your hand. You can offer your pets some of their food in your hand, but if they seem shy and nervous, leave them alone for a while or talk soothingly to them. Sometimes partially covering all but the front of their cage with a brown paper bag will help your mice feel more secure and less vulnerable as they will be able to detect less motion around their cage. Once they have become less nervous, you can completely remove the covering.

Housing Your Mice

The cage is the most expensive piece of equipment you will need to buy for your pet mice. The general rule when buying a cage is to choose the largest cage you can afford. The cage you choose should be a comfortable, roomy home for your mice. A cage that is too small and too confining will become dirty and smelly more quickly, and it can lead to fights among your pets because they may become grouchy without enough space. The more room that you provide your mice in which to play and explore, the more interesting and healthy they will be.

CHOOSING A CAGE

You can find a suitable cage for your mice at a pet store. Mice can be housed in glass aquariums, plastic cages, or in wire-frame cages. An ideal cage for a pair of mice should measure 20 inches long by 12 inches wide by 10 inches high. The rectan-

Whatever type of housing you provide for your mouse, it must be warm, dry, and clean.

gular plastic enclosures with snap-on lids, sometimes called small animal habitats, can be used to house a pair of mice as long as the habitat is large enough. These habitats are most suitable to use as carrying cages to take your mice home or to the veterinarian. They also provide a secure place to keep your pets while you are cleaning their cage. Be careful when cleaning these cages, as accidentally dropping them can cause them to break.

The cage you choose should be large enough to allow your mice room for separate eating, sleeping, and toilet areas. Most manufacturers label their cages for specific kinds of small pets, such as for mice or rabbits. In general, cages labeled for mice, hamsters, gerbils, and rats will provide suitable homes for pet mice.

Glass Aquarium Cages

A five- or ten-gallon glass aquarium with a secure, wire-screen cover will provide a good home for a pair of mice. Because mice can easily jump out of an aquarium, their cage must always be covered. Pet stores sell wire screens just for this purpose with latches to secure the top to the aquarium. Because the entire top lifts off the aquarium cage, pet owners are able to readily reach their pets. Compared to a wire-frame cage, an aquarium will keep the area around your pets' home tidy because shavings and other debris cannot spill out of the cage. However, the glass sides can become dirty and difficult to see through if they are not kept clean.

If you choose a glass aquarium or a plastic animal habitat, keep in mind that these types of housing are not as well-ventilated as a wire cage. While these cages are beneficial because they are not drafty, poor ventilation and lax cleaning habits can cause ammonia gas from your pets' urine to build up to uncomfortable levels. This can irritate your mice's respiratory system. For your pets' health, you must be vigilant in keeping such a cage clean. If you can smell your pets' home, then it is certainly an unhealthy environment for them, especially because they are right on top of the smelly bedding. If you think that you might be neglectful in cage-cleaning chores, select a wire-frame cage. Keep in mind that aquariums can be heavier than wire cages, and thus more difficult for a child to move and clean.

Wire-frame Cages

Wire-frame cages made of galvanized steel have good ventilation and offer a good view of your mice. While wire cages provide good ventilation, they are also potentially drafty. Mice like to climb and wire cages provide them with plenty of opportunities for gymnastics on the cage bars, especially in two or three story wire cages. Plain or colored metal cages are also available. These colored cages are often more attractive and can be

Wire-framed cages have good ventilation and offer a good view of you mouse. This lilac and tan female mouse has found another thing she likes about wire-framed cages— climbing to the top.

color-coordinated to match a room's décor. A good-quality wire-frame cage should be easy to clean with a slide-out or snap-off bottom tray.

If you house your mice in a wire-frame cage, make sure that there is a solid portion of the floor for the mice to stand and sit on. The metal wires can sometimes trap a mouse's foot, and constantly standing on the wire can make your pets' feet sore. You can place a small square of plastic or other non-chewable material on the bottom of the cage to add to your mice's comfort.

When you purchase the cage, check the tension on any springs for a snap-off bottom tray. Some springs are very tight and can be difficult for a child to undo to clean the cage. The cage should have a large door opening that allows you to easily reach inside the cage and take your mouse out. The door should have no sharp edges and should latch securely. The best cages will have both a door and a removable top or side to provide easy access to the interior of the cage. A handle can make moving the cage easier.

To prevent your pets from escaping, the space between the cage bars should measure no more than one-half an inch apart. This means that you cannot buy a larger cage made for rabbits, guinea pigs, or ferrets because the space between the bars will allow your mice to escape. If your mouse can squeeze his head between the cage bars, the rest of his body can follow. In such a case, temporarily attach a finer wire mesh (sold at hardware stores) to your pets' home until they grow too large to escape.

Metal cages do have some drawbacks. Over time, the mice's urine can corrode the metal pan that fits beneath a wire cage. You can help prevent this problem by cleaning your pets' bathroom area every few days or by lining the tray bottom with foil (as long as your mice do not have access to the tray). Plastic trays will not corrode from urine, but some mice will chew on the plastic if they can reach it.

If you choose a wire-frame cage, try to find one with high bottom tray sides to catch bedding and other debris that your mice will kick out during their normal activities. Alternatively, place the cage on top of newspaper that extends for several inches more than the cage's diameter, or you can place the cage inside a kitty litter pan to catch the material that spills out.

Other Types of Cages

Colorful plastic housing with connecting tubes allows you to expand your mice's cage into a playground. However, like aquariums, this type of housing provides less ventilation than wire cages. Tube housing can also become smelly if it is not cleaned frequently enough, and some mice can gnaw through the plastic tubes and escape. The plastic can also become dirty and difficult to see through, so it must be regularly washed. If you want tube housing for your mice, be sure to choose a large cage with maximum ventilation and a door that is large enough for you to reach in and easily take out your pets.

Some pet owners keep mice in unconventional cages, such as wire birdcages. Whatever cage style you choose, aquarium, plastic, wire, or unconventional, make sure the cage is escape-proof. Building a home for your mice can be a fun and creative project. However, do not build a cage out of wood. A wooden cage is not recommended because your pets can chew the wood and escape. In addition, wooden cages are difficult to keep clean because wood absorbs urine and other odors.

BEDDING

No matter what type of housing you buy, your mice need bedding in their cage. Bedding is used to absorb moisture (from urine, and water from the occasional leaking bottle), reduce odors, and provide a warm, dry place for your pets to sleep. Pet stores carry a variety of small animal beddings that are suitable for mice,

No matter what type of housing you choose for your mouse, you will need to provide some sort of bedding. You can use wood shavings or recycled paper that contains no inks or dyes.

Some bedding materials are better at controlling odor than others. These materials, however, usually cost more money.

including wood shavings such as pine and aspen, and more sophisticated beddings made from recycled paper or wood pulp that are designed to help control or eliminate odor. The latter types are more expensive, but they can make it more pleasurable to own mice since their home is less likely to smell unpleasant between cage cleanings. Bedding made from recycled paper contains no harmful inks, dyes, or significant levels of heavy metals. Whatever bedding you choose, you typically need only a few inches. The bedding should completely cover the wire floor of a wire cage.

Bedding is an important component of your pets' environment and it can affect their health. Ideally, small animal bedding should be dust-free. Dusty bedding can irritate a mouse's respiratory system or aggravate an existing respiratory ailment. Because mice are housed directly on their bedding, they are more likely to stir up fine particles and be at risk for these potential problems. In general, paper pulp and recycled paper products tend to be lower in dust than compared to wood shavings.

The Cedar Shavings Controversy

Shavings made from softwoods, which include pine and cedar, are still the most common type of bedding for small pets, such as mice. These beddings have been popular because they are relatively inexpensive and are often fragrant smelling. The pleasant smell associated with these materials is due to the aromatic compounds found in the wood. However, cedar shavings have been implicated as both causing and aggravating respiratory problems in small animals. In addition, they are known to affect liver function in rats and mice. Despite the controversy, few controlled, scientific studies have documented these problems. More common are reports that when a pet was removed from cedar shavings, its symptoms of poor health (such as sneezing) disappeared. Although not all experts agree that cedar shavings present a risk to small pets, a growing body of evidence seems to support hobbyists' contentions that cedar shavings can be unhealthy for small animals. Therefore, cedar shavings are not recommended for your mice.

Odor Control

The ammonia vapors from urine that develop in your pets' cage can make owning mice less than pleasant. The harsh smell is also uncomfortable for the mice. Ammonia is a severe irritant and is detrimental to the health of mice. It affects the mucous membranes of their eyes and respiratory tract. The health of mice can worsen if they are regularly exposed to ammo-

nia vapors, and it can make mice more susceptible to opportunistic infections. Mice housed on dirty, moist bedding are most susceptible to these effects, as are mice housed in aquariums that are infrequently cleaned.

The development of innovative bedding products has been spurred by the quest to control or eliminate odor. Scientifically developed bedding products made from a variety of materials, such as recycled paper, do not just mask odor, they are designed to reduce odor by controlling the formation of ammonia. Such beddings promote a healthier environment for mice compared with traditional wood shavings and are highly recommended. If your mice are housed in an aquarium, if you are neglectful in cage cleaning, or if family members despise your pets because they smell, use innovative, odor-controlling bedding.

CAGE ACCESSORIES

Place your mice's food in a dish. If you have a metal cage, you can attach the dish to the side to prevent your pets from tipping it over and spilling the contents. If you use a freestanding dish, make sure it is heavy enough that your mice cannot tip it over. Pet stores sell a variety of colorful ceramic dishes that are too heavy for mice to move. Mice are not always fastidious and some mice will go to the bathroom in their food dish. Because of this tendency, choose a smaller rather than a larger dish; your mice should not be able to stand in their food dish.

Provide your mice with fresh water, using a gravity-fed water bottle sold at pet stores. Water bottles sold for hamsters are a good size to use with mice. A special holder, also available at pet stores, enables you to hang the water bottle in an aquarium. Do not use an open dish to provide your mice with water. Mice will fill an open container of water with their bedding and droppings, and the water will become unsanitary and unsuitable for drinking. The increased moisture from a spilled dish of water can also create an unhealthy, damp environment, especially in an aquarium-type cage. In case the bottle leaks, do not place it over your pet's food dish or near their nest box. The bottle's water tube should be a comfortable height for your mice to reach up and drink from, but should not be so low to the cage floor that bedding could contact the tube and cause the bottle to leak.

Your mice need a nesting box for sleeping and security. Keep in mind that many pet stores do not provide nest boxes for their small pets because they want to make them easier for customers to see. Because the animals are only in the store for a brief period of time, no harm is done. A "bedroom" is necessary because it gives your mice a safe hiding place to retreat away from loud noises and any disturbing activity outside their

Place your mouse's food in a dish that is not too high for him to reach. Since some mice use their food dish to go to the bathroom, the dish should be large enough for food only.

Toys are a great way to keep your mouse occupied. Wooden ladders and platforms can give an ordinary cage another level for your mice to play on.

cage. You can buy a nest box at a pet store. A variety of types are sold, including ones that are made to satisfy a small animal's natural instinct to chew, such as fruit-flavored cardboard tunnels, huts made from natural plant fibers, and wooden blocks that a pet hollows out. Other kinds are less destructible and are made of ceramic or hard plastic. You can also make your pets a nest box from an old cereal box or cardboard milk carton. Once the box becomes chewed up or smelly, you will need to replace it.

Give your mice unscented tissue paper or paper towels to shred into nesting material. Shredding paper into a nest is a favorite activity among mice. Pet stores also sell nesting material that you can use. However, do not buy artificial fiber bedding sold for birds and hamsters. The small fibers can wrap around a mouse's feet, causing loss of the limb, and sometimes mice eat the material and cannot pass it out of their system.

Toys

Give your mice toys designed for hamsters, such as wooden chew sticks, tunnels, and ladders. Many wooden toys made for parakeets and parrots are also safe to use with your mice. Wood chews keep mice busy and active and provide a hard surface on which they can gnaw, which helps to keep their teeth in good shape. However, wooden objects will also absorb urine and other odors and will need to be replaced when they become smelly and old. If your pets are housed in an aquarium, you can increase the area available for your mice by adding ladders and platforms.

Mice will enjoy playing with almost anything you put in their cage. The greater the variety of toys, the more fun your mice will have and the more fun they are to watch. Mice enjoy running on exercise wheels and you should provide one for your pets. Freestanding wheels made of either plastic or metal are sold for use in aquariums or wire cages, or give your mice the cardboard rolls from empty toilet paper or paper towels. You can partially bury these tubes under your pets' bedding and create a system of tunnels for them to explore. Be creative, and connect multiple roles and make multiple entrances and exits.

Mice are agile climbers. A network of ropes strung through your pets' cage will provide hours of play. Cardboard egg cartons also provide entertaining play for mice. You can buy small mesh wire screen at a hardware store and construct various shapes to securely place in your pets' cage, but be sure that the wire edges are dull, not sharp. Your mice will enjoy crawling upside down and all over the screen.

WHERE TO KEEP THE CAGE

Your mice should be part of your family. Place their cage in a location where you can watch and enjoy them. Make the cage a pleasant part of the room. Place the cage on a dresser or table with some attractive fabric beneath it. The floor is not an ideal location, as the temperature near the floor is often cooler than on a dresser or table. On top of a high shelf is also not ideal, since it will be too high for you to enjoy your pets.

Do not place your pets' cage near a heating or air conditioning vent, a drafty window, or in direct sunlight. Mice are susceptible to over-heating, chills, and drafts. Mice can tolerate a house's normal variations in room light, temperature, and humidity. However, mice do not like bright lights, and strong lights can actually damage an albino mouse's pink eyes. Therefore, do not place your pets' cage next to a table, floor, or overhead light. Room temperatures between 65 – 85 degrees Fahrenheit (average 72 degrees) with humidity of 30 to 70 percent all provide satisfactory conditions. Mice that live in homes or cages outside these ranges will be stressed and are likely to become ill. Do not keep your pets in the garage. Not only is it an

Your mouse's housing should be located in a spot that is well-ventilated and draft-free.

unhealthy environment due to automobile exhaust, but the temperature is also more extreme and variable, and your pets are more likely to be neglected.

Your pets' cage should be placed out of the direct view of the family cat and dog. Your mice will be nervous and stressed if a dog or cat can constantly sniff and stare at them. Mice are also sensitive to the ultrasonic sounds produced by computers and televisions. Do not place your pets' home near either of these machines. Some experts recommend that you turn off a computer in a room housing pet mice when it is not in use. Doing so will further reduce any potential disturbance to your pets. Mice are enthusiastic gnawers. Do not leave any items such as clothing or papers on or near your pets' cage because anything that can be pulled into the cage will be chewed and destroyed.

CLEANING THE CAGE

A clean cage plays an important role in keeping your mice healthy. Plan on cleaning your pets' cage once or twice a week. The more mice kept in a cage, especially in a cage that is relatively small, the more often the cage will need to be cleaned. If, however, your pair of mice is housed in a very

If you are keeping more than one mouse, you need to make sure that the housing is large enough to give each mouse room. This cinnamon satin mouse and cinnamon mouse share the same housing.

THE GUIDE TO OWNING A MOUSE

This pied mouse is rummaging around in its bedding. Remember to change your mouse's bedding regularly to keep your mouse healthy.

large cage, such as a 20-gallon aquarium, then it is reasonable to consider cleaning the cage less often than twice a week.

Among pet hobbyists, mice are known for having a strong odor. Males in particular, have a "mousey" smell. A mouse's small, hard droppings do not smell bad, but their urine can develop a pungent ammonia smell. Ammonia is a severe irritant and is detrimental to the health of mice.

To clean your mice's cage, completely change the bedding in the cage and replace it with fresh, clean bedding. In between cleanings, you can do a partial cage change. Other types of small pets, such as gerbils and rats, will establish a toilet area in their cage, which can make cage cleaning easier. Some mice will designate a corner of their cage for a bathroom, but other mice will go everywhere. Try placing your mice's food dish, water bottle, and nest box at one end of their cage. This will help your mouse establish a bathroom area away from their sleeping and eating areas. If your pets do use a cage corner for a bathroom area, the bedding in this area can be replaced every few days or so. Doing so will help reduce odor and keep the cage cleaner and more sanitary. Each week, replace the nesting material in the mice's nest box. Less often, you will need to wash or replace some of your pets' toys and their nest box when they become chewed and tattered. Sometimes these objects absorb urine odors and become smelly. Replacing them, rather than washing them, will greatly decrease any pungent smell.

Some mice become upset and frantically run around their home after it has been cleaned. While pet owners find the clean cage refreshing, mice are not often as enthusiastic. They like something with their scent on it and will often become quite busy marking their home again so that is smells better to them. Partial cage cleanings, such as replacing some, but not all of your mice's bedding and nesting material, and not washing all of your pet's toys can satisfy your pets' need for something familiar.

Instead of feeling overwhelmed with the weekly task of cleaning and thus postponing it, try using a kitty litter scoop to quickly remove and replace some of the soiled bedding. Doing so can allow the cage to remain sanitary a few extra days before you undertake a more meticulous cleaning. Another way to make cage cleaning easier is to buy large quantities of bedding so you always have some around for a quick change.

Once a month, do a thorough cleaning. Wash the cage with hot, soapy water. Be sure to rinse and dry it thoroughly. If necessary, disinfect the cage with a bleach solution. Immersing a cage for at least 30 seconds in a bleach solution, consisting of one-tablespoon bleach for each gallon of cold water, will kill any germs. Allow the cage to air-dry afterward. Wash the water bottle, food dish, and any plastic toys. Wood toys can eventually splinter if washed in water, so scraping them clean with a file is effective. Scrape or file off any grime that might have accumulated on the bars of a wire cage.

You will need to place your pets in a secure container, such as a plastic carrying cage (small animal habitat) while you clean their home. Some mice owners place their pets in their nest box in the bathtub during cage cleaning. The nest box provides a secure hiding place and the slippery sides of the bathtub are usually too steep for mice to jump or climb out.

Feeding Your Mice

Feeding pet mice a healthy diet is easy because a variety of commercial foods are sold for mice at pet stores, usually sold in packages labeled for hamsters, gerbils, and mice. The dietary requirements for all of these rodents are similar, and foods sold for these pets will provide an adequate

Your mouse's basic diet of pelleted food can be supplemented with a variety of seeded treats.

diet for mice. Mice eat grains, seeds, fruits, berries, and nuts. Some mice will enjoy eating an occasional invertebrate, such as live mealworms, which you can buy at pet stores. When mice share people's homes, they will eagerly eat anything, including leftover meats such as steak, chicken, and ham, and cheese, for which they have a famous fondness.

Mice are fun to feed because they are adventurous and will eat practically anything you offer them, even foods that are not good for them, such as cookies and candy. It is up to you to provide your pets with a balanced and nutritious diet. Nutrition is a key factor in promoting good health and a long life. A mouse fed primarily junk food will not live as long as one that is fed a balanced diet.

A BALANCED DIET

A balanced diet for mice includes the appropriate amounts of protein, carbohydrate, fat, vitamins, and minerals. All these nutrients interact in the building, maintenance, and functioning of a mouse's body.

Because mice have been used as laboratory animals for so many years, a lot of reliable information exists on their nutritional needs. The amount of protein your pets need is influenced by a number of physiological factors, including age. Mice need less protein when they are adults than they do when they are growing, pregnant, or nursing a litter of babies. A good diet for a normal pet mouse should contain between 20 and 24 percent protein.

Fats are a significant source of calories and energy. A good diet for mice should contain approximately five percent fat. Fats make up part of the structure of every cell and are necessary for absorption of fat-soluble vitamins, including vitamins A, D, and E. Fats help to prevent and alleviate skin problems. A deficiency of fat can show up as scaly skin, or rough, thin hair. Carbohydrates are used as a source of energy. Your mice will easily get enough carbohydrates with a diet based on seeds and grains. Most seeds and grains are at least 50 percent carbohydrate.

Vitamins are necessary as catalysts for chemical reactions in the body. The vitamins that mice need to eat in their diet are different from those needed by people. For example, mice can make their own vitamin C, while people must get it from an external source, such as oranges. A number of vitamins, including many B vitamins, are synthesized in mice by intestinal bacteria. These vitamins are available to mice by means of coprophagy, which is when an animal eats special droppings that contain the vitamins synthesized by the bacteria. Mice typically engage in this behavior at night or early in the morning, when you are not likely to observe them.

It is easy to provide a mouse with a diet that is nutritious as well as varied. Just don't overfeed your mouse.

The mouse has survived throughout the centuries because it has been able to adapt to many different types of environments.

Nonetheless, do not be concerned if you see your pets engaged in such behavior. Leave them alone if you see your mice doing this, as coprophagy is necessary for their good health.

Mice require minerals and trace elements, such as iron, calcium, phosphate, and iodine. Minerals have many functions, from the structural role of calcium and phosphate in bones to the role of iron in bringing oxygen to the body. You can see what percentage of minerals is contained in some commercial mice foods by looking at the percentage of ash (ash is primarily minerals) listed under the guaranteed analysis. However, the percentage does not tell you exactly what minerals are present or in what amounts. Feeding your mice a fresh, high-quality diet will usually ensure adequate intake of necessary vitamins and minerals. Supplementation with a vitamin and mineral supplement, unless directed by your veterinarian, is unnecessary.

It is important that the food you feed your mice is fresh. Food that is old can become stale and lose some of its nutritional value. Packaged foods should be fresh and sweet smelling, not rancid or dusty. Do not buy a large amount of food because it will take too long to use all of it. Some manufacturers stamp a date on food bags and recommend that the food be used within one year of this date.

Proper storage of your mice's food is essential. Store your mice's food in a cool, dry environment. Sunlight, heat, and time will degrade the vitamins in a food, so keep your pets' food in an airtight container, such as a glass jar with a lid, or be sure to completely close a package that is self-sealing. This will keep the food fresh and prevent it from spoiling.

SUGGESTED DIETS

Feed your pets one of the rodent mixes sold at pet stores for mice, gerbils, and hamsters. These mixes contain seeds, grains, nuts, alfalfa pellets, and sometimes various type of kibble. Do not choose a food that is mostly sunflower seeds or other nuts, as such a diet will cause your mice to become overweight.

Mice enjoy picking through their food and eating their favorite items first. Since a food's nutritional analysis is based on consumption of the entire mix of ingredients, a selective eater may not be getting a nutritious, complete diet. Over time, this "selective feeding" can cause inadequate nutrition and obesity. While it is reasonable to expect your mice to dislike some items in their food, consistently refusing to eat more than half of a food's ingredients is not healthy.

Some mice breeders prefer to feed their pets only nutritionally complete laboratory blocks or pellets made specifically for mice and other

A good supplement to your mouse's diet is hay. Most mice enjoy tunneling through the hay before eating it.

rodents, or the breeders offer the lab blocks in addition to a rodent mix. These types of food contain a balance of all the nutrients your pets need. They are convenient and easy to feed. The ingredients in these blocks are blended so that a mouse cannot pick out one ingredient, and he will therefore consume adequate nutrients. Not all pet stores carry laboratory blocks, so you might have to ask them to special order the blocks if you want to offer them to your pets.

HOW MUCH TO FEED

You need to feed enough food to meet your mice's energy requirements. How much your mice need to eat will change throughout their lives, and the amount will vary according to your pets' age, gender, and activity level. Young, growing mice will need to eat more food per gram of body weight than do adults. Also, because male mice are larger than females, they need to eat more food than do females, although pregnant or nursing mice will need more food. Mice that are allowed to run around and play outside their cage will require more food than mice that just sit in their cage with little to do. Unless you weigh the amount of food you feed your pets, you are unlikely to notice these differences because they are very small.

Your mice should always have food in their dish. Even though they are primarily nocturnal, your mice will still nibble on food during the day. If your mice's dish is empty, increase the amount of food you feed your pets. Most mice will not overeat. Your mice should feel solid and sleek; they should not have large, bulging bellies. The amount your mice eat will vary depending on what type of food you feed. Typically, mice eat less of the laboratory blocks than they do of the rodent mixes.

It is best to feed your mice the same amount of food at the same time each day, such as when you come home from work or school, or when you have your own dinner. Since mice are nocturnal and most active at night, you should feed your pets in the evening rather than in the morning. Each day, you will need to discard the old food in their dish and replace it with fresh food.

The obvious satisfaction and delight that mice take when sorting through a fresh dish a food makes feeding a rewarding time to observe your pets. Watching your pets eat, even for a few minutes, will help you determine if they are active and well. Any marked loss or increase in a mouse's appetite could signal illness.

Some mice will store food in a corner of their cage, often hidden beneath some bedding. Check on their storeroom every once in a while to ensure that the food is not damp or moldy, and be sure to discard

Feeding bowls should always be clean. It would be wise to purchase bowls sturdy enough to prevent them from tipping and spilling food about.

stored food at each weekly cleaning. If your pets are housed in a wire cage, do not feed them through the cage bars. Otherwise, anything (including a finger) that is poked through the cage bars might get nipped. Always open the cage door to offer a treat. In addition, wash your hands before handling your mice in case any food smells on your hands entice your mice to nip.

TREATS

In addition to your mice's regular diet of grains, seeds, and laboratory blocks, you can offer your pets small amounts of fresh fruits and vegetables. Mice relish fruits and vegetables and can be given daily treats of small, well-washed pieces. Before offering these items, be sure to wash and dry them. Look at your mouse's front paws and use the size of his hands as a reasonable guide when deciding how much of a fresh food item to offer your pet. A mouse should be able to easily hold a piece of the diced fruit or vegetable between his hands. Leafy greens should be no more than about one by one inch in size. By using this conservative estimate of the amount, your pets are less likely to experience problems, such as diarrhea.

Offer your mice only one or two fresh items a day. The amount should depend on the type of food and whether your mice have eaten it before. Offer new foods in very small pieces to make sure your mice like it and to make sure it will not cause digestive upset (evidenced by diarrhea). Mice enjoy eating hard vegetables and fruits, such as carrots and apples, and are less likely to spoil than soft, moist items such as cucumbers and berries. Mice that regularly consume these items in their daily diet are less likely to experience digestive upset than mice that are rarely fed such foods. If you have not offered fruits or vegetables in a while, always err on the safe side by offering very tiny pieces.

Pay attention when feeding your mice their fresh food. Some mice will cart off and hide a piece of vegetable or fruit in their nest. If your mice do not eat their fresh food immediately it could spoil. Ideally, you should feed no more than your pets will consume right away. Every day, you will need to remove any uneaten fresh foods before offering your pets additional items. If there are constantly leftover fresh foods, you are probably feeding your mice too much and should reduce the amount you feed.

Pet stores also sell a variety of tasty treats for mice and other small rodents. Again, moderation is the key when feeding your mice treats. Your mice should not eat so many treats that they have no appetite for their regular food. Other treats to try offering your mice include dry, unsweetened cereals, pretzels, crack-

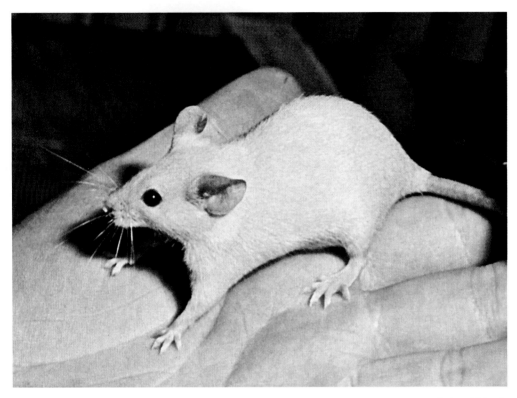

A well-balanced diet will be reflected in your mouse's appearance. Your mouse should look long and slender.

ers, stale bread, hard, uncooked noodles, uncooked rice, and uncooked, hot cereals (for example, cracked four-grain cereal). Many mice love dog biscuits, but be cautious when offering any of your dog's regular kibble because some brands are high in fat. These treats and the hard foods in your mice's regular diet will help to keep their teeth trim.

Some mice also enjoy eating live moths, mealworms, and crickets. Both crickets and mealworms are sold at pet stores for reptiles. It is fascinating to watch a mouse pounce on a mealworm or chase after and catch a cricket to eat. A mouse expertly turns a mealworm or cricket in his hands so that he consumes the head first before eating the remainder of the insect. Not all mice will eat live foods; some mice become frightened and want nothing to do with the insect. While some pet owners enjoy watching their mice eat live food, other people become squeamish. Live foods are not necessary; so do not worry if they are not your cup of tea. Conversely, avoid overindulging a mouse's appetite for live foods. Feed live foods as a treat only one or two every few days.

While it can be fun to offer your mice new types of food and see if they enjoy them, not all foods are good for mice. Do not feed your mice spoiled people food (for example, a sandwich found at the back of the fridge that has some mold) or junk food made for people. Although mice will greedily eat potato chips and eagerly look for more, potato chips, cookies, candy, and other snack foods are not healthy for your pets. Also avoid feeding high-protein, high-fat foods such as dry cat food and the seed and nut mixes sold for parrots and cockatiels

WATER

Your mice should always have water available. The amount of water mice drink each day depends on the moisture in their food, so if you provide your mice with small amounts of fresh fruits and vegetables, they will drink less water. The actual amount will vary depending on what you feed your mice. Monitor how much water your mice are drinking. If the amount of water in the bottle does not seem to decrease over a day or so, check to see if the metal spout is clogged with bedding.

Ideally, you should change your mice's water every day. However, most pet owners do not find this practical or convenient. At the very least, completely change the water in your mice's bottle once a week. It might be necessary to change the water more often if you have more than two mice in a cage. Select a water bottle that is large enough so that your mice do not run out of water. The standard hamster bottle provides sufficient water to last two mice for most of the week.

It is important to give the water bottle a good cleaning at least once a week. Even if the bottle looks clean, it is probably slimy on the inside and contaminated with bacteria and other harmful pathogens. Use a slender bristle brush to clean the slimy residue that will coat the bottle. Because some mice nibble the metal waterspout, check to be sure there are no jagged ends that could cut your mice. If there are, you should replace the water bottle.

Taming and Handling Your Mice

A tame mouse will let you hold him and pick him up without becoming frightened. The more time you spend holding and playing with your mice, the more quickly they will learn to trust you and become tame. It is best to begin your taming sessions in the early evening, when your mice are

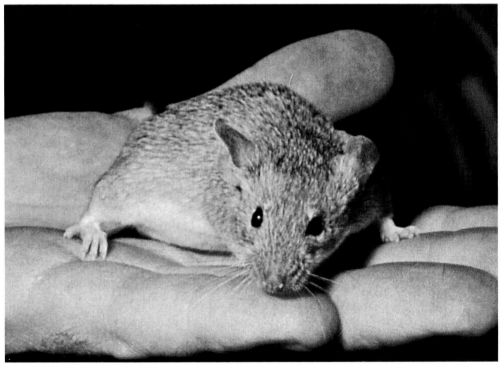

Until he gets comfortable being handled, do not hold your mouse too high as an unexpected leap may result in an injury.

naturally awake. If your mice are sleeping when you want to play with them, call their names, tap on their nest box, and allow them a few moments to wake up before you visit. If you startle or grab your pets, they might bite you. Do not force your pets to come out of their nest box when they would clearly rather sleep.

Some mice are very jumpy and active. If your pets' exhibit such behavior, it is best to start taming them by keeping your hand inside their cage, rather than taking your pets out of their cage. Let your mice sniff and crawl on your hand. Place a food treat in the palm of your hand and encourage them to climb onto your hand. Do not make rapid movements with your hands. If your mice seem confident, try using a finger to pet a mouse along his side or behind his ear. Even a brief momentary stroke will work. Continue to slowly pet your mice within their cage while talking softly to them so they get used to your voice. Eventually your pets will climb onto your hands. They might even climb out of the cage and up your arm. Replace the mice in their home before they get too far up your arm and they will renew their quest to explore outside their cage with renewed vigor and confidence.

HOLDING MICE

You can use one of several methods to pick up a mouse: (1) pick him up by scooping him into your hands; (2) pick him up by his tail; or (3) scoop him up in a small container. The preferred method to pick up your mouse is to let him climb onto your hand or to scoop him up under his belly. Mice can be frightened when a hand descends down over their back, so always put your hand in their cage palm up, lower it to the bottom of the cage, then move it toward your mouse. Do not turn him over on his back and expose his belly. This posture makes mice feel vulnerable, and they will become upset and will struggle frantically to right themselves. Keep in mind that a normally docile mouse might bite you when he is frightened.

You can use the base or middle of the mouse's tail to pick up your pet. Do not pick up your mouse by the end of his tail. Doing so is uncomfortable for the mouse, and your pet can turn and bite your finger, which will probably cause you to drop him. You can pick up your mouse by his tail, but you must be extremely gentle and you must immediately allow him to rest his body on your other hand or arm. Do not hold your mouse by his tail for longer than necessary. If you restrain your mouse by his tail he will struggle to try to get away. Instead, let him rest in one hand and use your other hand to block or control his movements. Never drop your mouse into his cage by his tail. Doing so could fracture his spine.

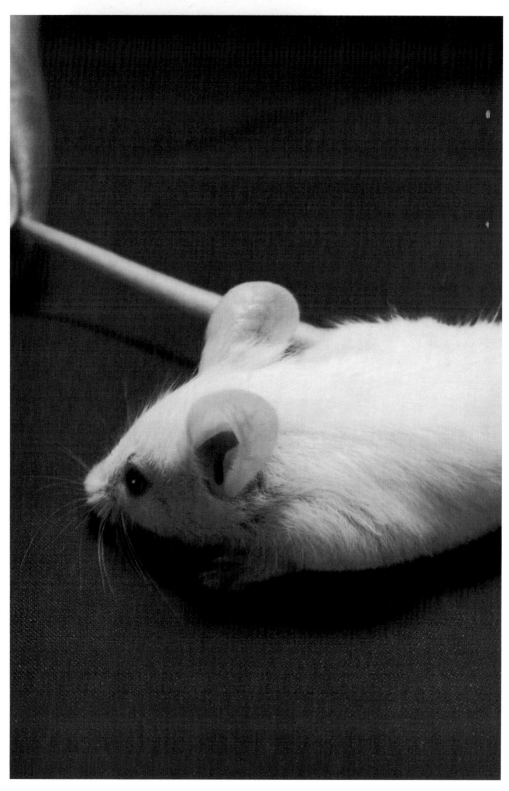

You should try not to pick up your mouse by his tail. If you must, let go of the tail as soon as possible.

Plastic toys for your mouse are a good investment. They are durable and easy to clean.

Mice do not like being scooped up in a container because containers usually have smooth sides that do not let the mouse hold onto anything. Nonetheless, this method may become useful in an emergency. Be sure the container you choose will easily fit into and out of the cage. Do not chase the mice around the cage with the container. Place the container on the cage floor near a corner and gently coax your mouse into the container. Cover the top of the container with one hand to prevent your mouse from leaping out.

Mice are nimble. Until your mouse is calm and tame, always use two hands to hold him. Loud noises and sudden movements (your own or those caused by another person or pet) could scare your pet and cause him to jump out of your hands. Use one hand to hold your mouse and lightly cup you other hand over his back or in front of his face. Keep your mouse close against your body for greater security. It is also prudent to immediately sit on the ground when first teaching a mouse to be held. Then, if he does jump, the distance is much less than if you were standing.

PLAYTIME

Mice are fun to watch while they play in their cage. However, most pet owners want to take their mice out of their cage to play. Doing so can be fun and beneficial because the more you play with your pets, the friendlier they will be. While other types of pets, such as rats, rabbits, and gerbils can be allowed to safely explore and play in a room, mice are too small for such an activity. The chances of their escaping and becoming lost are too great. Instead, think of yourself as your mice's playground. Let them play on you while you sit on a bed or a chair. Do not leave your pets unsupervised. Mice can quickly disappear into small nooks and crannies, and they will be very hard to find.

Other options for play outside your pets' cage include large plastic enclosures made especially for small pets that you can set up much like a child's playpen, a high-sided plastic swimming pool (at least 15 inches high), or a parrot play-stand. Place bedding, nest boxes, and toys in the playground. All these enclosures should be escape-proof. Plastic run-about-balls are another option. Be sure to choose the smaller, mouse-sized ball. Only one mouse can be placed in a run-about-ball at a time. Always supervise your pets. Stairs and other pets are potential hazards. Some balls are designed to move on a racetrack, which helps to confine your mice's movements to a safe place.

AN ESCAPEE

Should your mouse escape from his home, place the cage on the floor next to a wall. Do not leave the cage

Regular handling of your pet will prepare your mouse for shows should you plan to exhibit it. A quality show mouse will have a tail as long as its body.

TAMING AND HANDLING YOUR MICE

door open since your other mice will join the wanderer. Instead, provide the remaining mice with a new nest box, take the old nest box and the nesting material and place it on the floor next to the cage. Quite often, the mouse will return to the cage area and then fall asleep inside his familiar nest box.

INTRODUCING MICE TO EACH OTHER

If one of your mice dies and you want to get your remaining mouse a companion, you should follow these steps. Mice are territorial and often do not accept an unfamiliar mouse. Adult mice placed together in a cage for the first time will fight, sometimes until death. Remember, you can pair a male and a female, or two females, but not two males. If you had two brothers, and one died, do not try to pair your remaining male with another male, unless you pair him with a female.

A new cage is an unanticipated cost to purchasing a new mouse friend for your original pet. It is important that the cage or cages you use for the introduction be new. Your original mouse will resent any newcomer's intrusion into his territory. He will be aggressive in defense of his home and the chances of a successful introduction will be reduced. Buy a younger mouse to increase the

An escaped mouse will often return to the cage if you leave his nest box out next to the cage.

THE GUIDE TO OWNING A MOUSE

Mice are territorial and often do not accept an unfamiliar mouse in their cage. If you would like to get a new mouse, introductions should be made in a new cage and under close supervision.

chances for success. Younger mice tend to be more readily accepted than another adult.

Several methods can be used to facilitate the introduction. Place your original mouse in a wire cage, and place the new mouse in another wire cage. Slide the two cages together so the mice can smell one another through the cage bars. Alternatively, you can try dividing a wire cage or aquarium with a piece of wire mesh. You must be certain to securely place the wire so that the weight of a mice pressing against it will not cause the mesh to fall. If the mesh gives way, the mice could reach each other and they might fight. The spaces between the wire mesh should also be small enough that a mouse cannot push his nose through and bite the other mouse.

Over the next several days, switch the mice several times a day between the cages or sides of the cage. Usually the two mice will accept one another within several days. If they fight, you must continue switching them back and forth for several more days before once again housing them within the same cage. Carefully watch your mice for the first few days they share a home to make sure that they do not fight and have accepted one

A new mouse should be quarantined before being introduced to your other mice. A new mouse may be sick and pass the illness on to the others.

another. Any wounds from bites could indicate that the two mice are not getting along. Providing two nesting boxes for your mice can reduce the likelihood of the mice fighting.

QUARANTINE

An important caution about introducing a new mouse to your current pet is the potential risk of also introducing an illness. Serious hobbyists who breed mice usually quarantine a new arrival from their other mice, even if the newcomer seems healthy. A quarantine period helps prevent the transmission of illness among mice. The new arrival is kept in a cage as far away as possible from the other animals.

Pet owners rarely quarantine a new arrival, often because it means having to buy another cage and accessories. However, quarantining a new arrival is always the best approach. The quarantine period can last from two to four weeks. During this time, the new mouse's health is monitored. When the isolation period is over, the newcomer can be moved into the area containing the other mice, assuming it has exhibited no signs of ill health. If you purchased your new mouse from a serious breeder or a clean pet store, there is probably a low risk of any illness. Nonetheless, it is still a stressful time for all mice involved, and stress can cause mice to get sick.

Mouse Health Care

Knowing a mouse's normal behavior will help you recognize when one of your pets is sick. Experienced pet owners and breeders are adept at recognizing when a pet is sick. As you gain experience caring for your pets, especially if you develop a long-term interest, you will also become more

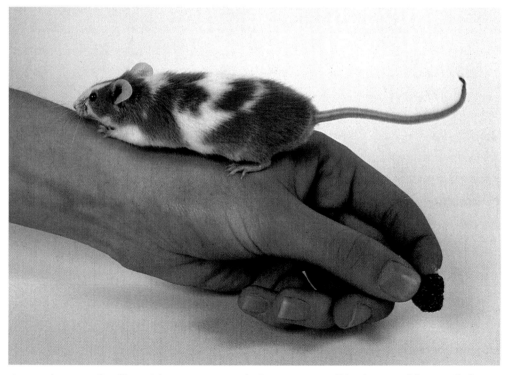

As you become familiar with your mouse's behavior, you will be better able to tell if your mouse is not feeling well.

proficient. Sick mice generally present a similar range of symptoms. Obvious signs of illness include discharge from the eyes or nose, sudden changes in behavior, lethargy, reduced appetite, and failure to groom. Signs of illness that are more difficult to detect include rough hair, hunched posture, and weight loss. You should pay particular attention to a mouse that is sensitive when touched on a certain part of his body, as this could indicate an injury from being dropped or squeezed. Any of these symptoms suggest that something might be wrong with your mouse and a visit to the veterinarian might be necessary.

Most mice that are sick need to be immediately treated by a veterinarian. This is especially important because pet owners often do not notice symptoms in their pet until the animal is very ill. By the time a pet owner realizes that something is wrong with his or her pet, the mouse has usually been sick for quite some time. In many cases, treatment is difficult because the condition usually is advanced at the time of detection. Although some diseases progress rapidly and an affected pet can suddenly die, early recognition of a sick mouse may mean the difference between life and death for your pet. Furthermore, keep in mind that the sicker a mouse is, the more likely he is to be traumatized from the procedures at a veterinarian's office.

Taking proper care of a sick mouse can help his recovery. Keep a sick pet in a warm, quiet area and monitor his water and food intake. Carefully administer any medications your veterinarian prescribes. During treatment, it might be necessary to quarantine a sick mouse from any other mice you have, especially if the ailment is contagious or your sick mouse needs quiet rest. Your veterinarian will let you know whether this is required.

FINDING A VETERINARIAN

In order for a mouse to receive the proper treatment, he needs the correct diagnosis. A veterinarian who routinely treats rodents and has a special interest in their care is best qualified and will most likely have the necessary, smaller-sized equipment to perform veterinary procedures. In order to locate a veterinarian who is knowledgeable about rodents, inquire at pet stores, critter clubs, and rescue societies.

Even when you recognize that your mouse is "under the weather," you might hesitate to take your pet to a veterinarian due to the potential expense. A visit to a veterinarian can be expensive, and it can be difficult to spend such large sums of money on a mouse.

Some mice owners will spend whatever it costs to treat their well-loved pets, but others are reluctant to do

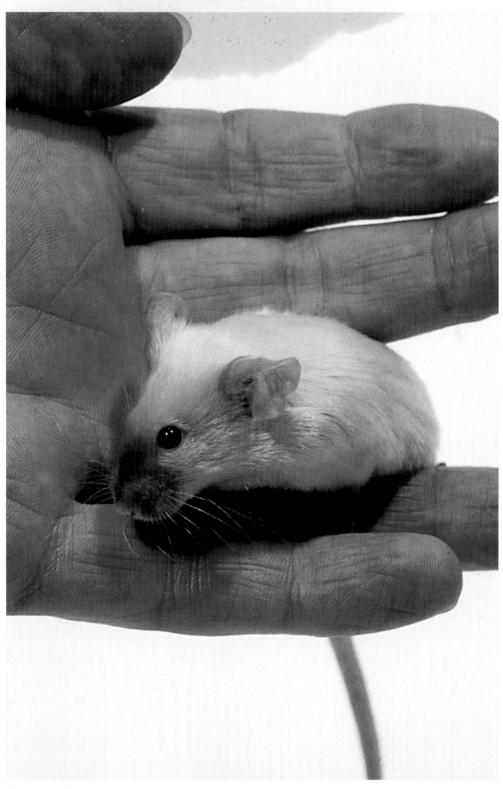

If you handle a sick mouse, wash your hands afterward to prevent passing on the illness to your other mice.

If you take the time and effort to properly feed and house your mouse, chances are it will be free from any infections and illness during its lifespan.

so. Discuss potential costs with your veterinarian beforehand, so you will have a better idea how much your mouse's care might cost. Although it might be difficult to put a price on your pet, in some cases, it might be necessary to decide how much you can afford to spend.

STRESS

Stress is a catch-all word for a variety of conditions that disturb or interfere with a mouse's normal physiological equilibrium. Because stress often leads to illness, it is frequently mentioned as a detrimental, contributing factor to various diseases. Besides becoming sick, a mouse can exhibit signs of stress in other ways, such as nervousness, lack of appetite, hair loss, and loose droppings.

It is useful for pet owners to be aware of what constitutes stress for their mice. A mouse can experience stress from pain and fear, moving to a new cage, a change in diet, and/or exposure to temperature fluctuations. The trip from a pet store or a breeder to a new home can be frightening and stressful for mice. Once in their new home, some mice settle down right away while others take longer to adjust. Other stressful situations include loud noises, changes in diet, overcrowding, and harassment by dogs, cats, ferrets, other pets, or other mice. Groups of mice housed together can fight and injure each other. Fighting and bullying is particularly stressful for the animal that is always picked on because it is at the bottom of the pecking order. Stress can be a major factor in the development of what might otherwise remain a dormant disease. Therefore, it is wise to minimize the stress in your mice's life.

ILLNESSES AND DISEASES

The ailments that might affect mice can be classified into five categories: (1) trauma-induced injuries, (2) infectious diseases, (3) noninfectious diseases, (4) improper husbandry, and (5) problems related to nutrition and aging. The reason why a mouse becomes sick is often a combination of factors from more than one category. For example, a poorly ventilated cage can create a noxious-smelling environment with high levels of ammonia that causes an outbreak of a latent respiratory disease. How sick the mouse will get also depends on the virulence of the pathogen, the mouse's age, dietary deficiencies, and whether the mouse is already sick with another illness.

Trauma-Induced Injuries

A traumatic injury is usually caused when a mouse is dropped, falls, or is squeezed while being held. If a mouse is injured, especially if he appears in pain, you should bring him to a veterinarian right away. The veterinarian can determine whether the

Practical management and good basic hygiene practices will go a long way to keeping your mice healthy.

injury can be treated or whether it would be kinder to end the mouse's suffering through euthanasia. Sometimes, some trauma injuries (such as injured toes) get better despite no care. However, broken bones are a potential hazard because mice can accidentally jump from your hands if something frightens them. Properly holding and playing with your mice can prevent such injuries from occurring.

Injuries from fighting among mice can also occur. This is most common when an unfamiliar mouse is introduced into a cage already occupied by other mice; thus this situation can usually be prevented by adhering to the previously discussed method of introducing mice.

Fighting mice will typically bite each other on the shoulder, rump, scrotum, and tail. Because infection from bacteria is always possible when a mouse is bitten in a fight, clean any bloody injuries with warm water and an antiseptic or hydrogen peroxide. An abscess can develop at the site of a bite wound due to bacterial infection. Watch the wounds, and if you detect any prolonged swelling, take your mouse to the veterinarian.

An abscess is usually due to a secondary bacterial infection from a bite wound inflicted during a fight, or it could be caused by the infection of a cut. Some experienced mice breeders are able to treat abscesses by using pressure to drain them. A veterinarian

Housing several mice in close quarters increases your pet's chances of contracting disease or infection. Make sure that the housing area is large enough for all of your mice.

MOUSE HEALTH CARE

Regularly handling your mouse will allow you to inspect for any abnormalities. If you notice something wrong, contact your vet and have your mouse looked at.

should tend to an abscess. Using a needle, the veterinarian will biopsy (or sample) the abscess, then drain and clean the site. Usually a topical antibiotic is applied to the area.

The bacteria that cause an abscess are often opportunistic and can infect other organs besides the skin. It is important that an affected mouse be properly treated. A veterinarian might deem it necessary to culture, or grow, a sample of the fluid to identify the type of bacteria present. An antibiotic selected on the basis of culture and sensitivity test results is likely to be highly effective.

Infectious Diseases

Infectious diseases can spread from one animal to another and are caused by bacteria, viruses, and protozoans. Sometimes the diseases caused by these agents are subclinical, with signs of infection difficult to detect. Individual animals also differ in their resistance to infectious organisms. Some exposed animals never display any symptoms. However, stress or other bacterial or viral infections can cause an animal to suddenly show symptoms. A single pet is less at risk for infectious diseases compared to a pet that is housed in close proximity to large numbers of other animals of the same species. Infectious diseases are often preventable through good husbandry.

Respiratory diseases are the most common infectious disease seen in mice. Symptoms include sniffling, sneezing, noisy breathing, and rough hair. If the inner ear becomes involved, the mouse will tilt his head. Respiratory diseases can be caused by bacteria, mycoplasmas, and viruses, often at the same time. Whatever the cause, respiratory diseases are contagious, and it is not possible to cure a sick mouse. A veterinarian can prescribe antibiotics that can relieve some symptoms, but the medication will not eliminate the infection. Young mice, old mice, mice sick from another ailment, and mice housed in dirty cages are particularly susceptible. Respiratory diseases can be fatal, and mice that live will often have chronic symptoms.

Noninfectious Diseases
Mites

Mice can sometimes be infested with mites, which are external parasites. Some mites are visible to the unaided eye, but others can only be seen under a microscope. Mites usually affect animals and do not typically affect pet owners. Symptoms of mite infestation include thinning hair, greasy coat, and scabs. For accurate diagnosis and treatment, your mice must be seen by a veterinarian who will identify the type of mites your mice are infected with, and prescribe the appropriate treatment. If you obtained your mice from a clean, reliable source, mites should not be a problem. Mites are spread by direct

Your mouse should be supervised at all times when he's out of his cage. Unsupervised play can lead to your mouse getting lost or injured.

contact between infested individuals or by infested bedding. Sometimes, an infestation of mites can be present for weeks or months before it becomes noticeable. If your mice suddenly appear to be infested by mites, and you use only good-quality, commercial bedding, you should suspect that your pets were previously infested.

Barbering

If you keep more than two mice together in a single cage, you might see a condition called barbering. A dominance hierarchy always forms among a group of mice. The dominant mouse bites or chews the muzzle and face of lower-ranked mice, which results in patches of lost hair and lost whiskers. Removing the dominant mouse, which usually has no bald areas, will help reduce this behavior. However, sometimes the next most dominant mouse will simply begin barbering the remaining cage occupants.

Tumors

Some types of tumors are benign, while others are a malignant form of cancer and will cause the death of an affected mouse. Tumors are seldom seen in young mice. More often, tumors occur in middle-aged and older mice. Mammary tumors are the most frequently seen type of tumor in mice. When playing with your pet, you might notice a swelling under the skin, which could be a tumor or abscess. If your mouse has a lump, you should consult a veterinarian to determine whether it is a tumor. Some tumors can grow quite large and will eventually interfere with a mouse's ability to move. A veterinarian can surgically remove a tumor, but the tumor will often reoccur. It is important to have a tumor removed early because large tumors can be more difficult to remove.

Malocclusion

Although not common, the teeth of some mice need veterinary attention due to malocclusion. Malocclusion occurs when a mouse's incisor teeth do not meet properly, either because the teeth are overgrown or they are misaligned. A mouse's teeth can fail to meet and wear properly for several reasons. Malocclusion can be inherited, or it can be caused by trauma, infection, or improper diet (for example, the mouse does not regularly eat foods hard enough to wear down his teeth). Even if you inspected the mouse's teeth before buying him, be aware that hereditary malocclusion is often not detectable in young mice. Even if the teeth appear normal at first, as the mouse grows, the teeth become misaligned.

Mice with this condition eventually cannot eat, lose weight, and will die without treatment. Many show symptoms often referred to as "slobbers," which are threads of saliva around the mouth and sometimes wiped on the front paws. If you notice that your pet is not eating, you can check his incisors by pulling back his lips. An affected mouse should be taken to a veterinarian who will clip or file the mouse's teeth.

Improper Husbandry

When properly cared for, mice are less stressed and have better natural resistance to diseases. A plethora of problems can affect mice due to poor husbandry. Husbandry is a big word for how a pet is taken care of and includes aspects such as housing, food, and water. A mouse is completely dependent upon you to provide it with the proper environment because mice cannot modify the size, temperature, air circulation, and cleanliness of their home. Providing a spacious, clean cage is one of the most important ways you can help your mice stay healthy.

With proper care and nutrition, your mouse will live a happy and healthy life as your pet.

Spoiled food and a dirty cage are invitations for illness. Routine cleaning is the most effective method to prevent disease organisms from becoming established in your mice's home and overpowering their natural resistance to disease. Your mice are most likely to get sick when you become forgetful about cleaning their cage.

Small pets such as mice often seem to tolerate a dirty environment, but their tolerance will eventually diminish and they will become ill if kept in an unsanitary environment.

Problems Related to Aging and Nutrition

Some mice are allergic to peanuts. Symptoms of peanut allergy are scabs on the mouse's head and shoulders due to excessive scratching. A veterinarian can confirm the scabs are not caused by a mite infestation. Eliminating peanuts from the mouse's diet will eventually result in the complete healing of the scabs.

Age

As a mouse gets older, you might begin to notice changes in his behavior and body condition due to aging. Symptoms often appear gradually in old animals so that pet owners sometimes do not notice. However, middle-aged and older mice are more prone to illnesses than when they were young. Noninfectious ailments such as tumors and cataracts are usually seen in older mice. Depending on their heredity, some old mice become skinny while others have a tendency to gain weight. Old mice also groom themselves less frequently, thus their fur no longer looks as sleek and shiny.

Considering whether to euthanize an old mouse is very painful. Your veterinarian can help you with this decision. The time to discuss this option is when your mouse is no longer able to leave his nest box, must be force fed, or is terminally ill. In some cases, it might be better for a mouse to be painlessly put to sleep rather than being subjected to stressful treatment that would add only a few weeks to a mouse's life.

Zoonotic Diseases

Parents are sometimes concerned about whether mice can give their children an illness, especially because children often forget to wash their hands after playing with their pets. Zoonotic diseases are diseases that can be transmitted from animals to people. Pet mice present few potential health problems to people. Some pet owners develop allergies, such as a skin rash, to mice dander and urine. The potential for disease transmission is reduced with proper hygiene, such as washing your hands after playing with your pets and keeping their cage clean. Purchasing your mice from a clean environment rather than a smelly, dirty one further reduces the chance of a mouse having a zoonotic disease.

Resources

ORGANIZATIONS

American Fancy Rat and Mouse Association
9230 64th Street
Riverside, CA 92509-5924
(626) 966-0350
E-mail: rattusrat@hotmail.com
www.afrma.org

American Pet Mouse and Hamster Owners and Breeders
John Jones
P.O. Box 610
Douglas City, CA 96024
Phone: (916) 778-0240
E-mail: johnpaul@snowcrest.net

American Rat, Mouse, and Hamster Society
C/o Denise Boyce
8275 Westmore Road #30
San Diego, CA 92126
Phone: (619) 390-2903
Fax: (619) 390-5271
www.altpet.net/rodents/rats/ARMHS.html

Rat and Mouse Club of America
13075 Springdale St PMB 302
Westminster, CA 92683
E-mail: RMGazette@aol.com
www.rmca.org/

Rat, Mouse, and Hamster Fanciers
C/o Silvia Butler
188 School Street
Danville, CA 94526
E-mail: Jstarkey@telis.org

INTERNET RESOURCES

Animal Hospitals—USA
www.animalhospitals-usa.com/small_pets/gerbils.html

Electronic Zoo/ Net Vet—Rodents
http://netvet.wustl.edu/rodents.htm

Pet Finder
www.petfinder.org

RESCUE AND ADOPTION ORGANIZATIONS

The American Society for the Prevention of Cruelty to Animals
424 East 92nd Street
New York, NY 10128-6801
(212) 876-7700
www.aspca.org
E-mail: information@aspca.org

The Humane Society of the United States (HSUS)
Companion Animals Section
2100 L Street, NW
Washington, DC 20037
(202) 452-1100
www.hsus.org

EMERGENCY SERVICES

Animal Poison Hotline
(888) 2320-8870

ASPCA Animal Poison Control Center
(888) 426-4435
www.aspca.org

Index

Photo Credits

Isabelle Francais, Michael Gilroy, Eric Jukes, Rodney Luedtke, and Vince Serbin